THE ROYAL
HORTICULTURAL
SOCIETY

DIARY
2023

First published in 2022 by Frances Lincoln Publishing, an imprint of The Quarto Group.
The Old Brewery, 6 Blundell Street
London, N7 9BH
United Kingdom
www.Quarto.com

With thanks to Helen Bostock, RHS Senior Horticultural Advisor, Andrew Salisbury, RHS Principal Scientist Entomology and Richard Dee, RHS Horticultural Taxonomist.

A catalogue record for this book is available from the British Library.

ISBN 978 0 7112 7169 2

10 9 8 7 6 5 4 3 2 1

Printed in China

Title page *Malva moschata*, early 19th century, by Lydia Penrose

Below *Crocus flavus* subsp. *flavus* 'Lutescens', 1847, by William Herbert

RHS FLOWER SHOWS 2023
The Royal Horticultural Society holds a number of prestigious flower shows throughout the year. At the time of going to press, show dates for 2023 had not been confirmed but details can be found on the website at: rhs.org.uk/shows-events

Every effort is made to ensure calendarial data is correct at the time of going to press but the publisher cannot accept any liability for any errors or changes.

CALENDAR 2023

JANUARY
M	T	W	T	F	S	S
						1
2	3	4	5	6	7	8
9	10	11	12	13	14	15
16	17	18	19	20	21	22
23	24	25	26	27	28	29
30	31					

FEBRUARY
M	T	W	T	F	S	S
		1	2	3	4	5
6	7	8	9	10	11	12
13	14	15	16	17	18	19
20	21	22	23	24	25	26
27	28					

MARCH
M	T	W	T	F	S	S
		1	2	3	4	5
6	7	8	9	10	11	12
13	14	15	16	17	18	19
20	21	22	23	24	25	26
27	28	29	30	31		

APRIL
M	T	W	T	F	S	S
					1	2
3	4	5	6	7	8	9
10	11	12	13	14	15	16
17	18	19	20	21	22	23
24	25	26	27	28	29	30

MAY
M	T	W	T	F	S	S
1	2	3	4	5	6	7
8	9	10	11	12	13	14
15	16	17	18	19	20	21
22	23	24	25	26	27	28
29	30	31				

JUNE
M	T	W	T	F	S	S
			1	2	3	4
5	6	7	8	9	10	11
12	13	14	15	16	17	18
19	20	21	22	23	24	25
26	27	28	29	30		

JULY
M	T	W	T	F	S	S
					1	2
3	4	5	6	7	8	9
10	11	12	13	14	15	16
17	18	19	20	21	22	23
24	25	26	27	28	29	30
31						

AUGUST
M	T	W	T	F	S	S
	1	2	3	4	5	6
7	8	9	10	11	12	13
14	15	16	17	18	19	20
21	22	23	24	25	26	27
28	29	30	31			

SEPTEMBER
M	T	W	T	F	S	S
				1	2	3
4	5	6	7	8	9	10
11	12	13	14	15	16	17
18	19	20	21	22	23	24
25	26	27	28	29	30	

OCTOBER
M	T	W	T	F	S	S
						1
2	3	4	5	6	7	8
9	10	11	12	13	14	15
16	17	18	19	20	21	22
23	24	25	26	27	28	29
30	31					

NOVEMBER
M	T	W	T	F	S	S
		1	2	3	4	5
6	7	8	9	10	11	12
13	14	15	16	17	18	19
20	21	22	23	24	25	26
27	28	29	30			

DECEMBER
M	T	W	T	F	S	S
				1	2	3
4	5	6	7	8	9	10
11	12	13	14	15	16	17
18	19	20	21	22	23	24
25	26	27	28	29	30	31

CALENDAR 2024

JANUARY
M	T	W	T	F	S	S
1	2	3	4	5	6	7
8	9	10	11	12	13	14
15	16	17	18	19	20	21
22	23	24	25	26	27	28
29	30	31				

FEBRUARY
M	T	W	T	F	S	S
			1	2	3	4
5	6	7	8	9	10	11
12	13	14	15	16	17	18
19	20	21	22	23	24	25
26	27	28	29			

MARCH
M	T	W	T	F	S	S
				1	2	3
4	5	6	7	8	9	10
11	12	13	14	15	16	17
18	19	20	21	22	23	24
25	26	27	28	29	30	31

APRIL
M	T	W	T	F	S	S
1	2	3	4	5	6	7
8	9	10	11	12	13	14
15	16	17	18	19	20	21
22	23	24	25	26	27	28
29	30					

MAY
M	T	W	T	F	S	S
	1	2	3	4	5	
6	7	8	9	10	11	12
13	14	15	16	17	18	19
20	21	22	23	24	25	26
27	28	29	30	31		

JUNE
M	T	W	T	F	S	S
					1	2
3	4	5	6	7	8	9
10	11	12	13	14	15	16
17	18	19	20	21	22	23
24	25	26	27	28	29	30

JULY
M	T	W	T	F	S	S
1	2	3	4	5	6	7
8	9	10	11	12	13	14
15	16	17	18	19	20	21
22	23	24	25	26	27	28
29	30	31				

AUGUST
M	T	W	T	F	S	S
			1	2	3	4
5	6	7	8	9	10	11
12	13	14	15	16	17	18
19	20	21	22	23	24	25
26	27	28	29	30	31	

SEPTEMBER
M	T	W	T	F	S	S
						1
2	3	4	5	6	7	8
9	10	11	12	13	14	15
16	17	18	19	20	21	22
23	24	25	26	27	28	29
30						

OCTOBER
M	T	W	T	F	S	S
	1	2	3	4	5	6
7	8	9	10	11	12	13
14	15	16	17	18	19	20
21	22	23	24	25	26	27
28	29	30	31			

NOVEMBER
M	T	W	T	F	S	S
				1	2	3
4	5	6	7	8	9	10
11	12	13	14	15	16	17
18	19	20	21	22	23	24
25	26	27	28	29	30	

DECEMBER
M	T	W	T	F	S	S
						1
2	3	4	5	6	7	8
9	10	11	12	13	14	15
16	17	18	19	20	21	22
23	24	25	26	27	28	29
30	31					

Plants for Pollinators

The *Royal Horticultural Society Diary 2023* features beautiful botanical illustrations from the RHS Lindley Collections – the world's largest collection of botanical art – highlighting the essential role of plants for pollinators.

The artworks included illustrate some of the many plants for pollinators and are by a variety of talented artists. Among those that appear within these diary pages is Pierre-Joseph Redouté (1759–1840). Belgian-born Redouté achieved success as a painter working for the French royal court tutoring Marie Antoinette. From 1798 he was appointed to paint the flowers of Malmaison by Joséphine Bonaparte.

Also featured is Caroline Maria Applebee (c.1799–1854). Born in England, Applebee appears to have been the daughter of a wealthy middle-class family that had conservatories and greenhouses providing access to the plants and flowers she painted.

Pollinators are a vital part of a healthy vibrant garden. Any insect that visits a flower to feed on or collect nectar and pollen can carry out pollination. By moving from flower to flower, they pollinate many garden and wild flowers and are essential for the cropping of most fruits and some vegetables.

Bees are just some of the thousands of flower-visiting insects. There are hundreds of species of hoverfly, and hundreds if not thousands of other flies, social and solitary wasps, beetles, butterflies and moths. Worryingly, bees and other pollinators are considered to be in decline. Though gardens already support a

wide range of pollinators, with a little thought, gardeners can introduce an even wider variety and help to reverse this trend.

A good way to encourage pollinators into your garden is by growing nectar- and pollen-rich flowers throughout the year. To aid gardeners in selecting flowers that support pollinators, the RHS has created the *Plants for Pollinators* list. The list is based on scientific evidence, the extensive experience of RHS staff and the records of gardeners, and contains a range of year-round flowers that can help tackle the decline in pollinator numbers. Please visit www.rhs.org.uk/plantsforpollinators for plant suggestions by month.

You can also support pollinators by:
- Allowing lawn 'weeds' to flower by cutting less often
- Providing water for pollinators
- Avoiding using pesticides wherever possible and never spraying open flowers
- Providing nest sites for bumblebees and solitary bees
- Tolerating some nibbled leaves and greenflies – these can be food for larval stages of some pollinators such as hoverflies and moths.

DECEMBER/JANUARY

26 *Monday*

27 *Tuesday*

28 *Wednesday*

29 *Thursday*

30 *Friday*   *First quarter*

31 *Saturday*   New Year's Eve

01 *Sunday*   New Year's Day

Fuchsia coccinea, 1827–1833, by Pierre-Joseph Redouté

JANUARY

Holiday, UK, Republic of Ireland,
USA, Canada, Australia and New Zealand
(New Year's Day)

Monday 02

Holiday, Scotland and New Zealand

Tuesday 03

Wednesday 04

Thursday 05

Full moon
Epiphany

Friday 06

Saturday 07

Sunday 08

Salvia rosmarinus, date unknown, by Ferdinand Lukas Bauer

JANUARY

09 Monday

10 Tuesday

11 Wednesday

12 Thursday

13 Friday

14 Saturday

15 Sunday

Last quarter

Wood cranesbill (*Geranium sylvaticum*), 1814, by Caroline Maria Applebee

JANUARY

Holiday, USA (Martin Luther King Jnr Day)

Monday 16

Tuesday 17

Wednesday 18

Thursday 19

Friday 20

New moon

Saturday 21

Chinese New Year

Sunday 22

Bomarea formosissima, 1808, by Johann Simon Kerner

JANUARY

23 Monday

24 Tuesday

25 Wednesday

26 Thursday   Holiday, Australia (Australia Day)

27 Friday

28 Saturday   First quarter

29 Sunday

Myosotis scorpioides, 1827–1833, by Pierre-Joseph Redouté

JANUARY/FEBRUARY

Monday 30

Tuesday 31

Wednesday 01

Thursday 02

Friday 03

Saturday 04

Full moon

Sunday 05

Dog rose (*Rosa canina*), early 19th century, by Lydia Penrose

FEBRUARY

06 Monday

Accession of Queen Elizabeth II
Holiday, New Zealand (Waitangi Day)

07 Tuesday

08 Wednesday

09 Thursday

10 Friday

11 Saturday

12 Sunday

Oxe-eye daisy (*Leucanthemum vulgare*), early 19th century, by Lydia Penrose

FEBRUARY

Last quarter

Monday **13**

Valentine's Day

Tuesday **14**

Wednesday **15**

Thursday **16**

Friday **17**

Saturday **18**

Sunday **19**

Paeonia tenuifolia, 1827–1833, by Pierre-Joseph Redouté

FEBRUARY

20 Monday

New moon
Holiday, USA (Presidents' Day)

---

21 Tuesday

Shrove Tuesday

---

22 Wednesday

Ash Wednesday

---

23 Thursday

---

24 Friday

---

25 Saturday

---

26 Sunday

Dahlia, 1809, by Caroline Maria Applebee

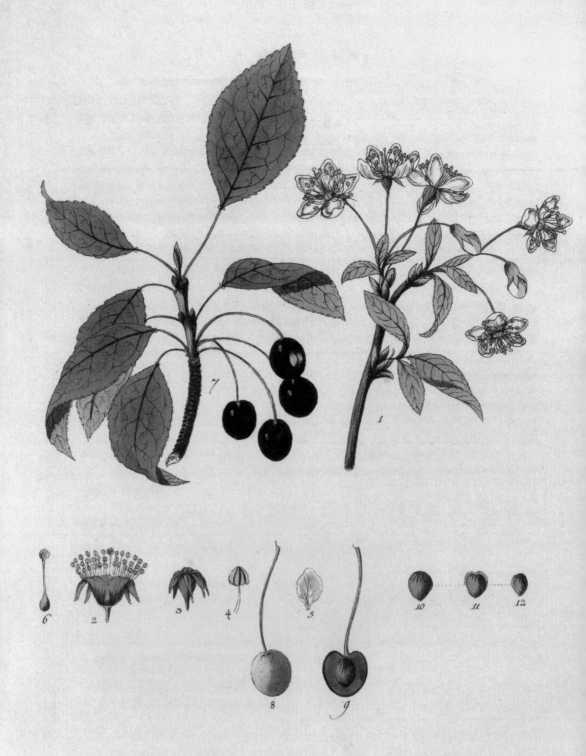

FEBRUARY/MARCH

First quarter   Monday 27

Tuesday 28

St David's Day   Wednesday 01

Thursday 02

Friday 03

Saturday 04

Sunday 05

Wild cherry tree (*Prunus avium*), 1786, by Johann Simon Kerner

06 *Monday*

07 *Tuesday*   *Full moon*

08 *Wednesday*

09 *Thursday*

10 *Friday*

11 *Saturday*

12 *Sunday*

Viburnum tinus, 1840, by Caroline Maria Applebee

MARCH

Commonwealth Day | *Monday* **13**

Tuesday **14**

Last quarter | *Wednesday* **15**

Thursday **16**

St Patrick's Day
Holiday, Republic of Ireland
and Northern Ireland | *Friday* **17**

Saturday **18**

Mothering Sunday, UK and Republic of Ireland | *Sunday* **19**

Tropaeolum majus variety, 1827–1833, by Pierre-Joseph Redouté

MARCH

---

20 *Monday*

Vernal Equinox (Spring begins)

---

21 *Tuesday*

New moon

---

22 *Wednesday*

---

23 *Thursday*

First day of Ramadân
(subject to sighting of the moon)

---

24 *Friday*

---

25 *Saturday*

---

26 *Sunday*

British Summer Time begins

Box shrub (*Buxus sempervirens*), 1792, by John Frederick Miller

Male

Female

MARCH/APRIL

Monday 27

Tuesday 28

First quarter

Wednesday 29

Thursday 30

Friday 31

Saturday 01

Palm Sunday

Sunday 02

Papaver rhoeas, 1824, by John Curtis

APRIL

03 Monday

04 Tuesday

05 Wednesday

06 Thursday

Full moon
Maundy Thursday
First day of Passover (Pesach)

07 Friday

Good Friday
Holiday, UK, Canada, Australia
and New Zealand

08 Saturday

09 Sunday

Easter Sunday

Cornflower (*Centaurea cyanus*), 1791, by John Frederick Miller

Easter Monday
Holiday, UK (exc. Scotland), Republic of Ireland,
Australia and New Zealand

Monday 10

Tuesday 11

Wednesday 12

Last quarter

Thursday 13

Friday 14

Saturday 15

Sunday 16

Ratibida pinnata, 1815, by James Sowerby

APRIL

17 *Monday*

18 *Tuesday*

19 *Wednesday*

20 *Thursday*

New moon

21 *Friday*

Birthday of Queen Elizabeth II
Eid al-Fitr (end of Ramadân)
(subject to sighting of the moon)

22 *Saturday*

23 *Sunday*

St George's Day

Meadow cranesbill (*Geranium pratense*), 1826, by Caroline Maria Applebee

2   3   4

APRIL

Monday 24

Holiday, Australia and New Zealand
(Anzac Day)

Tuesday 25

Wednesday 26

First quarter

Thursday 27

Friday 28

Saturday 29

Sunday 30

Paeonia daurica, 1813, by Pierre-Joseph Redouté

MAY

---

01 *Monday*

Early Spring Bank Holiday, UK
Holiday, Republic of Ireland

---

02 *Tuesday*

---

03 *Wednesday*

---

04 *Thursday*

---

05 *Friday*

Full moon

---

06 *Saturday*

---

07 *Sunday*

Digitalis grandiflora, c.1790–1818, by Ferdinand Lucas Bauer

MAY

Monday 08

Tuesday 09

Wednesday 10

Thursday 11

Last quarter

Friday 12

Saturday 13

Mother's Day, USA, Canada,
Australia and New Zealand

Sunday 14

Allium ampeloprasum, 1802–1816, by Pierre-Joseph Redouté

MAY

---

15 *Monday*

---

16 *Tuesday*

---

17 *Wednesday*

---

18 *Thursday* Ascension Day

---

19 *Friday* *New moon*

---

20 *Saturday*

---

21 *Sunday*

Veronica speciosa, 1847, by Caroline Maria Applebee

a   b   c

MAY

Holiday, Canada (Victoria Day)   Monday 22

Tuesday 23

Wednesday 24

Thursday 25

Feast of Weeks (Shavuot)   Friday 26

First quarter   Saturday 27

Whit Sunday   Sunday 28

Zinnia elegans, 1798, by Johann Simon Kerner

MAY/JUNE

29 *Monday*

Spring Bank Holiday, UK
Holiday, USA (Memorial Day)

30 *Tuesday*

31 *Wednesday*

01 *Thursday*

02 *Friday*

Coronation Day

03 *Saturday*

04 *Sunday*

Full moon
Trinity Sunday

Alstroemeria pelegrina, 1802–1816, by Pierre-Joseph Redouté

JUNE

Holiday, Republic of Ireland
Holiday, New Zealand (The Queen's Birthday)

Monday 05

Tuesday 06

Wednesday 07

Corpus Christi

Thursday 08

Friday 09

Last quarter
The Queen's Official Birthday
(subject to confirmation)

Saturday 10

Sunday 11

Siberian larkspur (*Delphinium grandiflorum*) and varieties of marguerite (*Argyranthemum frutescens*), 1820, by Caroline Maria Applebee

JUNE

12 *Monday*   Holiday, Australia (The Queen's Birthday)

13 *Tuesday*

14 *Wednesday*

15 *Thursday*

16 *Friday*

17 *Saturday*

18 *Sunday*
New moon
Father's Day, UK, Republic of Ireland,
USA and Canada

Héliotrope du Pérou (*Heliotropium arborescens*), c.1800, artist unknown

JUNE

Holiday, USA (Juneteenth)

Monday 19

Tuesday 20

Summer solstice (Summer begins)

Wednesday 21

Thursday 22

Friday 23

Saturday 24

Sunday 25

Eschscholzia californica, 1816, by Caroline Maria Applebee

JUNE/JULY

26 Monday   *First quarter*

27 Tuesday

28 Wednesday

29 Thursday

30 Friday

01 Saturday   Canada Day

02 Sunday

Helleborus, c.1660s, by Nicolas Robert

JULY

Full moon
Holiday, Canada (Canada Day)

Monday 03

Holiday, USA (Independence Day)

Tuesday 04

Wednesday 05

Thursday 06

Friday 07

Saturday 08

Sunday 09

Fuchsia magellanica var. *gracilis* 'Versicolor', 1843, by Caroline Maria Applebee

JULY

10 Monday

Last quarter

---

11 Tuesday

---

12 Wednesday

Holiday, Northern Ireland (Battle of the Boyne)

---

13 Thursday

---

14 Friday

---

15 Saturday

St Swithin's Day

---

16 Sunday

Rosa stylosa, 1820, by John Lindley

JULY

New moon   Monday 17

Tuesday 18

Islamic New Year   Wednesday 19

Thursday 20

Friday 21

Saturday 22

Sunday 23

Penstemon, 1832, by Caroline Maria Applebee

JULY

24 Monday

25 Tuesday   *First quarter*

26 Wednesday

27 Thursday

28 Friday

29 Saturday

30 Sunday

Greater common bistort (*Persicaria bistorta*), 1791, by John Frederick Miller

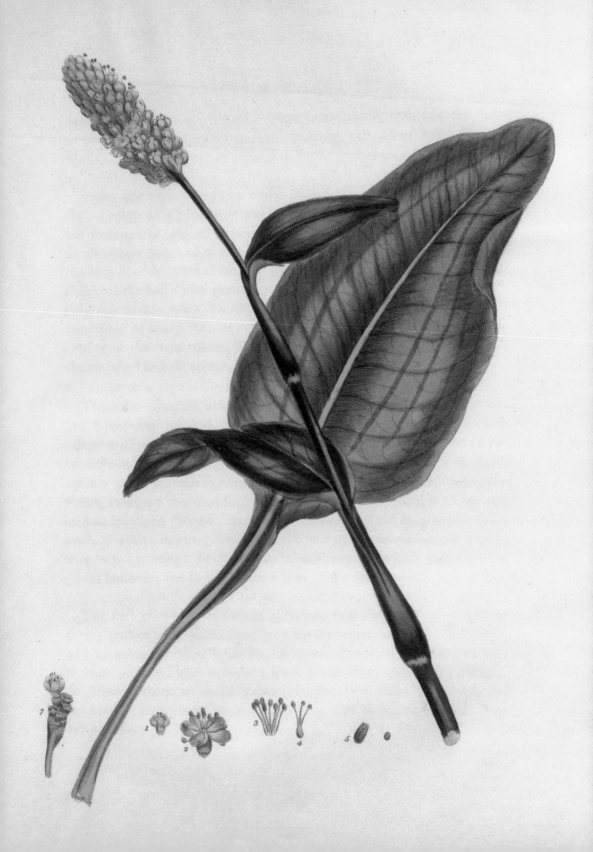

JULY/AUGUST

Monday 31

Full moon

Tuesday 01

Wednesday 02

Thursday 03

Friday 04

Saturday 05

Sunday 06

Lupinus nanus and *Fuchsia magellanica*, 1844, by Caroline Maria Applebee

AUGUST

07 *Monday* Holiday, Scotland and Republic of Ireland

08 *Tuesday* *Last quarter*

09 *Wednesday*

10 *Thursday*

11 *Friday*

12 *Saturday*

13 *Sunday*

Rosa moschata, 1805–1828, by Henry Charles Andrews

AUGUST

Monday **14**

Tuesday **15**

New moon

Wednesday **16**

Thursday **17**

Friday **18**

Saturday **19**

Sunday **20**

Ail rose (*Allium roseum*), 1802–1816, by Pierre-Joseph Redouté

AUGUST

21 Monday

22 Tuesday

23 Wednesday

24 Thursday   *First quarter*

25 Friday

26 Saturday

27 Sunday

Ramson garlic (*Allium ursinum*), early 19th century, by Lydia Penrose

Summer Bank Holiday, UK
(exc. Scotland)

Monday 28

Tuesday 29

Wednesday 30

Full moon

Thursday 31

Friday 01

Saturday 02

Father's Day, Australia and New Zealand

Sunday 03

Alstroemeria ligtu, 1802–1816, by Pierre-Joseph Redouté

SEPTEMBER

---

04 Monday

Holiday, USA (Labor Day)
Holiday, Canada (Labour Day)

---

05 Tuesday

---

06 Wednesday

Last quarter

---

07 Thursday

---

08 Friday

---

09 Saturday

---

10 Sunday

Wallflower (*Erysimum cheiri*), early 19th century, by Lydia Penrose

SEPTEMBER

Monday 11

Tuesday 12

Wednesday 13

Thursday 14

New moon

Friday 15

Jewish New Year (Rosh Hashanah)

Saturday 16

Sunday 17

Blackberry (*Rubus fruticosus*), 1847, by Caroline Maria Applebee

SEPTEMBER

18 Monday

19 Tuesday

20 Wednesday

21 Thursday

22 Friday

First quarter

23 Saturday

Autumnal Equinox (Autumn begins)

24 Sunday

Penstemon murrayanus, 1841, by Caroline Maria Applebee

SEPTEMBER/OCTOBER

Day of Atonement (Yom Kippur)　　　　　　　　　　　　　　　　*Monday* 25

Tuesday 26

Wednesday 27

Thursday 28

Full moon
Michaelmas Day　　　　　　　　　　　　　　　　　　　　　　*Friday* 29

First day of Tabernacles (Succoth)　　　　　　　　　　　　　*Saturday* 30

Sunday 01

Paeonia × suffruticosa 'Pak Mou Tan', c.1819, artist unknown

OCTOBER

02 *Monday*

03 *Tuesday*

04 *Wednesday*

05 *Thursday*

06 *Friday*   *Last quarter*

07 *Saturday*

08 *Sunday*

Blackberry (*Rubus fruticosus*), 1792, by John Frederick Miller

OCTOBER

Holiday, USA (Columbus Day)
Holiday, Canada (Thanksgiving)

Monday 09

Tuesday 10

Wednesday 11

Thursday 12

Friday 13

New moon

Saturday 14

Sunday 15

Galanthus nivalis, 1802, by Johann Stephan Capieux

OCTOBER

16 Monday

17 Tuesday

18 Wednesday

19 Thursday

20 Friday

21 Saturday

22 Sunday

First quarter

Delphinium elatum, c.1680, by Frans George Beissner

OCTOBER

Holiday, New Zealand (Labour Day)   Monday **23**

Tuesday **24**

Wednesday **25**

Thursday **26**

Friday **27**

Full moon   Saturday **28**

British Summer Time ends   Sunday **29**

Crataegus monogyna, 1814, by Caroline Maria Applebee

OCTOBER/NOVEMBER

30 *Monday* — Holiday, Republic of Ireland

31 *Tuesday* — Halloween

01 *Wednesday* — All Saints' Day

02 *Thursday*

03 *Friday*

04 *Saturday*

05 *Sunday* — *Last quarter*
Guy Fawkes Night

Honeysuckle (*Lonicera periclymenum*), early 19th century, by Lydia Penrose

NOVEMBER

Monday 06

Tuesday 07

Wednesday 08

Thursday 09

Holiday, USA (Veterans Day)

Friday 10

Veterans Day, USA
Remembrance Day, Canada

Saturday 11

Remembrance Sunday

Sunday 12

Common thyme (*Thymus vulgaris*), 1739, by Elizabeth Blackwell

NOVEMBER

13 *Monday*   *New moon*

14 *Tuesday*

15 *Wednesday*

16 *Thursday*

17 *Friday*

18 *Saturday*

19 *Sunday*

Crocus imperati, 1847, by William Herbert

NOVEMBER

First quarter

Monday 20

Tuesday 21

Wednesday 22

Holiday, USA (Thanksgiving)

Thursday 23

Friday 24

Saturday 25

Sunday 26

Digitalis grandiflora, 1821, by John Lindley

27 Monday

Full moon

---

28 Tuesday

---

29 Wednesday

---

30 Thursday

St Andrew's Day

---

01 Friday

---

02 Saturday

---

03 Sunday

First Sunday in Advent

Sorbus aucuparia, 1785, by Johann Simon Kerner

DECEMBER

Monday 04

Last quarter   Tuesday 05

Wednesday 06

Hannukah begins (at sunset)   Thursday 07

Friday 08

Saturday 09

Sunday 10

Escallonia rubra, 1842, by Caroline Maria Applebee

DECEMBER

11 Monday

12 Tuesday

New moon

13 Wednesday

14 Thursday

15 Friday

Hannukah ends

16 Saturday

17 Sunday

Dahlia, 1809, by Caroline Maria Applebee

DECEMBER

Monday 18

First quarter

Tuesday 19

Wednesday 20

Thursday 21

Winter Solstice (Winter begins)

Friday 22

Saturday 23

Christmas Eve

Sunday 24

Digitalis purpurea, 1821, by Ferdinand Lukas Bauer

DECEMBER

---

25 *Monday*

Christmas Day
Holiday, UK, Republic of Ireland, USA, Canada,
Australia and New Zealand

---

26 *Tuesday*

Boxing Day (St Stephen's Day)
Holiday, UK, Republic of Ireland, USA, Canada,
Australia and New Zealand

---

27 *Wednesday*

Full moon

---

28 *Thursday*

---

29 *Friday*

---

30 *Saturday*

---

31 *Sunday*

New Year's Eve

Holly (*Ilex aquifolium* 'Argentea Marginata'), 1833, by Caroline Maria Applebee

YEAR PLANNER

JANUARY	JULY
FEBRUARY	AUGUST
MARCH	SEPTEMBER
APRIL	OCTOBER
MAY	NOVEMBER
JUNE	DECEMBER